Questions and Answers: Countries

Finland

A Question and Answer Book

by Donald B. Lemke

Consultant:
Tom DuBois
Department of Scandinavian Studies
University of Wisconsin
Madison, Wisconsin

Capstone
press

Mankato, Minnesota

Fact Finders is published by Capstone Press,
151 Good Counsel Drive, P.O. Box 669, Mankato, Minnesota 56002.
www.capstonepress.com

Library of Congress Cataloging-in-Publication Data
Lemke, Donald B.
    Finland : a question and answer book / by Donald B. Lemke.
    p. cm.—(Fact finders. Questions and answers. Countries)
    Summary: "Describes the geography, history, economy, and culture of Finland in a
    question-and-answer format"–Provided by publisher.
    Includes bibliographical references and index.
    ISBN 0–7368–4355–8 (hardcover)
    1. Finland—Juvenile literature. I. Title. II. Series.
DL1012.L46 2006
948.97--dc22   2005001168

Editorial Credits
Silver Editions, editorial, design, and production; Kia Adams, set designer; Ortelius Design,
Inc., cartographer; Wanda Winch, photo researcher; Scott Thoms, photo editor

Photo Credits
Art Directors/N. Price, 16–17
Aurora/Look/Ingolf Pompe, 10–11, 13
Aurora/Bilderberg/Wolfgang Kunz, cover (background)
Capstone Press Archives, 29 (bill, coins)
Comma Image Ltd, cover (foreground), 15, 18–19, 20, 21, 23, 25, 26–27
Corbis/Chris Lisle, 4
Corel, 1
Getty Images Inc./Time Life Pictures/Mark Kauffman, 7
One Mile Up, Inc., 29 (flag)
Photo courtesy of the Parliament of Finland/Matti Bjorkman, 9

Artistic Effects:
Brand X Pictures/Steve Allen, 8
Photodisc/C Squared Studios, 16; John A. Rizzo, 24

1 2 3 4 5 6 10 09 08 07 06 05

Table of Contents

Features

Where is Finland?

Finland is located in northern Europe. It is a little smaller than the U.S. state of New Mexico. Part of Finland is in the Arctic. The area is often cold.

There are many lakes and forests in Finland. More than 190,000 lakes are found across the country. Forests grow around many of these lakes.

Forests of pine, spruce, and birch trees surround many of Finland's lakes.

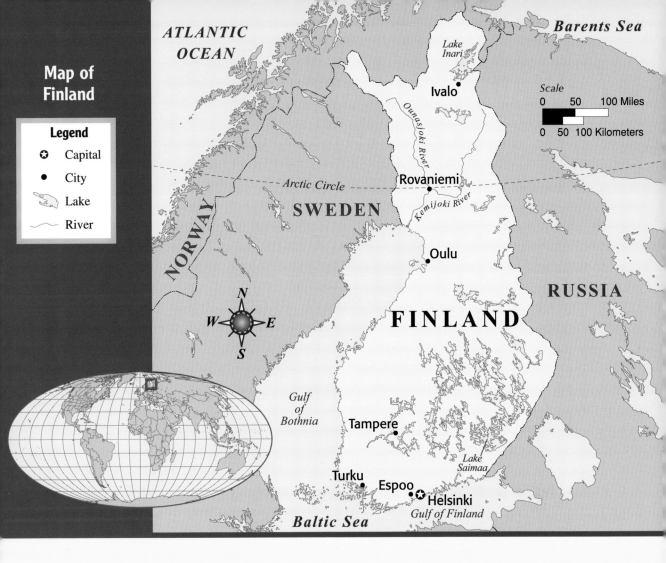

Lake Saimaa is the fifth largest lake in
Europe. It covers about 1,700 square miles
(4,380 square kilometers).

Finland's waters have thousands of
islands. Many are found off the southern
coast. Some of them are national parks.

When did Finland become a country?

Finland became a country on December 6, 1917. On that day, the government declared independence from Russia. After two years of political struggle, Finns elected Kaarlo Juho Ståhlberg as the first president.

Hundreds of years earlier, Sweden and Russia fought for the area of Finland. Sweden ruled the area from the 1200s to the 1800s. In 1809, Russia defeated Sweden in the Finnish War (1808–1809). Russia stayed in control of Finland until 1917.

Fact!

The Winter War with the Soviet Union lasted from 1939 to 1940. During the war, many Finnish soldiers traveled on skis.

In 1949, Finnish and Soviet officials met to sign a final peace treaty.

On November 30, 1939, the Soviet Union attacked Finland. During the Winter War (1939–1940), Finland survived against a much larger Soviet army. After World War II (1939–1945), the Soviet Union and Finland finally signed a peace agreement.

What type of government does Finland have?

Finland's government is a **democratic republic**. People elect a president and representatives to run the country.

Like the U.S. government, Finland's government has three branches. They are the executive branch, the legislative branch, and the judicial branch.

Fact!

Finland joined the European Union in 1995. The 25 European Union countries promote peace and business success with each other.

Finland's 200 legislative members meet regularly at the Parliament House in Helsinki.

The president and **prime minister** are the executive branch. The prime minister helps the president run the country. Members of the legislative branch make the laws of Finland. The Supreme Court and lower courts are part of the judicial branch. They help explain the country's laws.

What kind of housing does Finland have?

People in Finland live in apartments and houses. Most housing is located in the southwestern part of the country. In cities, many people live in apartment buildings. In rural areas, people live in small homes. Many Finns also own vacation homes near lakes or the southern coast.

Where do people in Finland live?

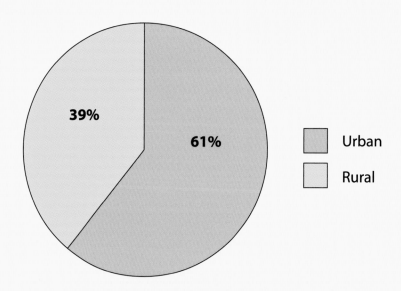

39%

61%

Urban

Rural

Poorvo, one of Finland's oldest cities, has many vacation homes near its lake.

In Finland, most houses and apartments have a **sauna**. Saunas are small, wooden rooms. The rooms are filled with hot air that is dry or steamy. After Finns sit in the sauna, they sometimes roll in snow or jump in a lake to cool off.

What are Finland's forms of transportation?

Finns use many forms of transportation. Many people own cars. In cities, Finns often ride buses, trains, and subways. People also walk or ride bikes. During winter, some people ski to work on special trails.

Many Finns fly around the country on airplanes. The largest airport is located in the capital, Helsinki.

Fact!

In the past, people in northern Finland traveled on sleighs pulled by reindeer. Today, tourists can ride on reindeer sleighs for fun.

Ferries crossing the Gulf of Finland carry people and cars.

Finns also travel by ferry boat. People can drive their cars onto ferry boats. These boats carry people across lakes. They also take people to islands off the coast. In winter, ferries are often replaced by roads across frozen lakes or seas.

What are Finland's major industries?

Finns work in service and manufacturing jobs. Many service people work with tourists, in stores, or in banks. Manufacturing workers make many goods.

Finland is known for making communication products. Finland is one of the largest makers of cell phones in the world. The phones are sold in Finland and to other countries.

What does Finland import and export?	
Imports	**Exports**
grains	communication products
iron	machinery
petroleum	paper

Timber from forests is used in the paper and pulp industries.

Finland has many thick forests. Workers cut down trees to make wood and paper. Finland **exports** more paper than any country except Canada.

What is school like in Finland?

Children in Finland start school when they are 7 years old. They must stay in school for nine years. They study math, science, history, music, and languages. All students learn Finnish and Swedish. Many students also learn English.

Fact!

All children in Finland must take music classes until they are 14 years old.

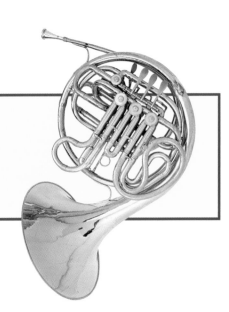

Skiing is a popular after-school sport in Finland.

INARIN ALA-ASTE
ANÁRA VUOLLEDÁSSI

After nine years of school, some students go to upper secondary schools. They get ready for college at these schools. Other students go to **vocational school** to learn how to do a job. Vocational schools last for three years.

What are Finland's favorite sports and games?

Finns enjoy playing outside. In the winter, people go cross-country skiing. In the summer, they like to hike, fish, and swim. Others compete in **orienteering** events.

Soccer is a favorite sport in Finland. The country has a national men's team and a national women's team. Many Finnish children play soccer with friends.

Fact!

Pesäpallo *is Finland's national sport. This sport is like baseball in the United States.*

Children enjoy playing a game of ice hockey in Lānge Imāki.

Ice hockey is another popular team sport. People cheer for the national team. In 1995, Finland won the gold medal at the World Ice Hockey Championships.

What are the traditional art forms in Finland?

For hundreds of years, Finns have made up stories, poems, and songs. Many of these were not written down. In the 1800s, Elias Lönnrot traveled around Finland. He listened to poetry and songs and wrote them down. He put them in a book called the *Kalevala*. Today, people can read the book in almost 50 different languages.

The kantele is the oldest folk instrument in Finland.

An orchestra plays at a festival in Helsinki.

Finns also like to listen to music. More than 30 **orchestras** play around the country.

The kantele is the national instrument of Finland. It has between five and 32 strings. Musicians sit down to hold the kantele. They pluck the strings with their fingers.

What major holidays do people in Finland celebrate?

Midsummer is one of Finland's most famous holidays. Midsummer is the day of the year when the sun stays out the longest. It stays light almost all night. Many families travel to their summer homes on this holiday. They listen to music, dance, and light **bonfires**.

On December 6, Finns celebrate Independence Day with parades. They also light candles and place them on graves.

What other holidays do people in Finland celebrate?

Easter
Mother's Day
New Year's Day
Vappu (May Day)

Finns enjoy celebrating Midsummer festival in Parainen.

On Christmas Eve, many families eat holiday meals and rest in saunas. In the evening, Finnish children wait for gifts from Father Christmas, also called Santa Claus. Some people believe Santa Claus lives in Rovaniemi in northern Finland.

What are the traditional foods of Finland?

People in Finland enjoy many types of meat, fish, and vegetables. Many Finns eat elk and reindeer. They also enjoy beef and pork. Finns serve potatoes and other vegetables with most meals.

Finns eat many types of fish and seafood. Salmon and herring are favorites. In summer, people love to eat crayfish.

Fact!

People in Finland drink more coffee than anywhere else in the world.

These Finns enjoy sharing a meal of salmon and crayfish.

Finns also enjoy fruit and wild berries. In spring, strawberries and blueberries grow across the country. Small, yellow berries called cloudberries grow in the north. Cloudberries look like raspberries and taste like apples.

What is family life like in Finland?

Many Finns wait until they are older to start a family. They need to save money before having children. Both men and women have jobs. They share the cost of paying for a house.

Families in Finland are smaller than they used to be. Most families now have one or two children.

What are the ethnic backgrounds of people in Finland?

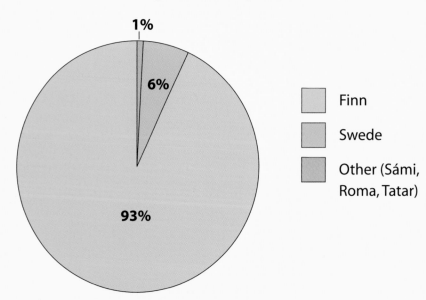

1%

6%

93%

Finn

Swede

Other (Sámi, Roma, Tatar)

A young family spends time together cross-country skiing.

Both parents usually keep their jobs after having children. The government lets at least one working parent stay home during a child's first year. After this time, young children stay with grandparents or at day care.

Finland Fast Facts

Official name:

Republic of Finland

Land area:

*117,552 square miles
(304,473 square kilometers)*

**Average annual
precipitation:**

26 inches (66 centimeters)

**Average January
temperature (Helsinki):**

*21 degrees Fahrenheit
(minus 6.1 degrees Celsius)*

**Average July
temperature (Helsinki):**

*62 degrees Fahrenheit
(16.8 degrees Celsius)*

Population:

5,214,512 people

Capital city:

Helsinki

Languages:

Finnish and Swedish

Natural resources:

*copper, iron ore, silver,
timber, zinc*

Religions:

Evangelical Lutheran	*89%*
Orthodox	*1%*
None	*9%*
Other	*1%*

Money and Flag

Money:

Finland's money is called the euro. In 2005, 1 U.S. dollar equaled 0.77 euro. One Canadian dollar equaled 0.61 euro.

Flag:

Finland's flag was chosen on May 29, 1918. The background stands for the white snow of winter. The blue cross stands for the country's many lakes.

Learn to Speak Finnish

Most people in Finland speak Finnish. It is one of Finland's official languages. Learn to speak some Finnish words using the chart below.

English	Finnish	Pronunciation
hello	hyvää päivää	(HEW-vah PY-vah)
How are you?	Mitä kuuluu?	(MEE-tah KOO-loo)
nice to meet you	hauska tavata	(HOUS-kah TOWH-vah-tah)
good morning	hyvää huomenta	(HEW-vah HOO-OH-men-tah)
good night	hyvää yötä	(HEW-vah OO-OH-tah)
sorry	anteeksi	(AHN-tayk-see)
thank you	kiitos	(KEEH-tohs)

Glossary

bonfire (BON-fire)—a large outdoor fire

democratic republic (dem-uh-KRAT-ik ri-PUHB-lik)—a government headed by a president or prime minister with officials elected by voters

export (EK-sport)—to send and sell goods to other countries

orchestra (OR-kuh-struh)—a large group of musicians who play their instruments together

orienteering (or-ee-uhn-TIHR-ing)—a sport in which people have to find their way across rough country as fast as they can, using a map and compass

prime minister (PRIME MIN-uh-stur)—the person in charge of a government in some countries; Finland's prime minister is chosen by the president.

sauna (SAW-nuh)—a bath using dry heat, or a steam bath in which the steam is made by throwing water on hot stones; saunas began in Finland.

vocational school (voh-KAY-shuhn-ul SKOOL)—a school that trains students for a job

Internet Sites

FactHound offers a safe, fun way to find Internet sites related to this book. All of the sites on FactHound have been researched by our staff.

Here's how:
1. Visit *www.facthound.com*
2. Type in this special code **0736843558** for age-appropriate sites. Or enter a search word related to this book for a more general search.
3. Click on the **Fetch It** button.

FactHound will fetch the best sites for you!

Read More

Hutchinson, Linda. *Finland.* Modern Nations of the World. San Diego: Lucent Books, 2004.

Yip, Dora. *Welcome to Finland.* Welcome to My Country. Milwaukee: Gareth Stevens, 2002.

Zhong, Meichun. *Finland.* Countries of the World. Milwaukee: Gareth Stevens, 2001.

Index